CHILDREN
OF THE HOLOCAUST

Alex Woolf

BARRON'S

First edition for North America published
in 2014 by Barron's Educational Series, Inc.

First published in 2014 by Franklin Watts

Copyright © Franklin Watts, 2014

Franklin Watts
338 Euston Road, London, NWI 3BH

Franklin Watts is a division of Hachette
Children's Books, a Hachette U.K. company.
www.hachette.co.uk

Editor: Sarah Ridley

Editor in chief: John C. Miles

Designer: Jane Hawkins

Picture researcher: Diana Morris

All inquiries should be addressed to:
Barron's Educational Series, Inc.
250 Wireless Boulevard
Hauppauge, NY 11788
www.barronseduc.com

ISBN: 978-0-7641-6758-4

Library of Congress Control Number:
2014940649

Date of Manufacture: July 2014
Manufactured by: South China Printing Co.,
Dongguan City, China

Printed in China
9 8 7 6 5 4 3 2 1

The publisher and author would like to acknowledge the following permissions:

The following testimonies are reproduced by kind permission of the Imperial War Museum © Imperial
War Museums (sound description): Ruth Foster (page 7), John Silberman (7 and 9), Sergei Hackel (8),
Gisela Eisner (8), Gerda Williams (9), John Lawrence (11), Herbert Elliott (11), Josef Perl (11), Susan
Sinclair (12 and 13), John Richards (13 and 14), Hedy Epstein (14), Jerry Koenig (16, 18, and 28), Ezra
Jurmann (17), Janina David (18 and 19), Roman Halter (21, 42, and 55), Marsha Segall (22), Ryvka
Salt (23 and 52), Edyta Klein-Smith (24), Stanley Faull (25 and 49), Alicia Adams (31), Daniel Ivin (38),
Barbara Stimler (40), Helen Pelc (41), Jan Hartman (41, 48, and 51), John Fink (42), Alfred Huberman
(43), Clare Parker (44), Taube Biber (44), Anna Bergman (47), Michael Honey (49), Zdenka Ehrlich
(50–51), Harry Lowit (51), Kitty Hart-Moxon (53), and Rina Quint (54).

Gerda Klein's testimony on pages 16–17 is reproduced by kind permission of her son
James A. Klein.

The following testimonies are reproduced by kind permission of United States Holocaust Memorial
Museum: Emanuel Tanay, Shulamit Perlmutter (Charlene Schiff) (pages 19 and 26), Elizabeth Kaufman
Koenig (page 39) and David Levine (pages 26–27).

Sabina Zimering's testimony on page 35, from her memoir *Hiding in the Open*, is reproduced by kind
permission of the publishers, North Star Press of St. Cloud.

Hedi Fischer Frankl's testimony on pages 37, 41, and 43 is reproduced by kind permission of the author.

The testimonies of Tova Friedman (page 45) and Frieda Tennenbaum (page 46), from *Kinderlager:
An Oral History of Young Holocaust Survivors* (Holiday House), are reproduced by kind permission of the
book's author, Milton Nieuwsma.

Helga Weiss's testimony (pages 47–48) was originally published in *Guardian* and is reproduced with
their consent.

The testimonies of Krystyna Chiger (27), Richard Rozen (31 and 35), Renee Roth-Hano (32) and Rosa
Sirota (32–33), from *The Hidden Children: The Secret Survivors of the Holocaust* by Jane Marks, published
in the U.K. by Piatkus (an imprint of Little, Brown Book Group) and in the U.S. by Ballantine Books, are
reproduced by kind permission of the publishers.

Every attempt has been made to contact the copyright holders of quoted materials. Should any
references have been omitted, please contact the publisher, who will endeavour to correct the
information in subsequent editions.

CONTENTS

CHAPTER 1

WHAT WAS THE HOLOCAUST?

THE HOLOCAUST WAS THE MASS MURDER OF AROUND SIX million Jews. It was carried out by the German Nazi Party during World War II. The Nazis also killed other groups, including Roma and Sinti people, Slavs and homosexuals, but by far the largest group of victims were the Jews. By the end of the Holocaust, well over half the Jewish population of Europe—one-third of all the Jews in the world—had been killed.

WHY DID IT HAPPEN?

The Nazis, led by Adolf Hitler, were racists who believed that the Germanic peoples (who they called Aryans) were superior to all other peoples. They saw the Jews as their "racial enemies." Shortly after the Nazis came to power in Germany in 1933, they began passing laws to strip German Jews of their civil rights.

KRISTALLNACHT

On the night of November 9–10, 1938, the persecution of German Jews became violent. The Nazis organized pogroms (anti-Jewish riots) throughout Germany. Jews were attacked, and thousands of Jewish homes, businesses, and synagogues were damaged or destroyed. It became known as *Kristallnacht* (Crystal Night) because it left the streets covered in broken glass (see page 12). From 1938, Nazi Germany began invading its neighboring countries, and Jews throughout Europe came under threat.

Adolf Hitler was a failed Austrian painter who rose to become leader of the Nazi Party and the Chancellor of Germany from 1933 to 1945. In the 1920s, Hitler wrote a memoir, *Mein Kampf* (My Struggle), in which he talks of a Jewish conspiracy to take over the world.

◄ Over a million of those who died in the Holocaust perished here at Auschwitz-Birkenau, a network of camps that operated between 1941 and 1945 in Nazi-occupied Poland.

GHETTOS AND CONCENTRATION CAMPS

With the outbreak of World War II in 1939, the Nazis began moving hundreds of thousands of Jews into very small, overcrowded areas of cities called ghettos. They weren't allowed to leave and many died of starvation and disease. The Nazis also set up giant prisons called concentration camps where Jews and others were often tortured and worked to death.

THE FINAL SOLUTION

Some time in 1941, the Nazi leaders agreed on what they called "the final solution of the Jewish question." They decided to exterminate the Jewish people. In 1942, the Nazis built six extermination camps in Poland, complete with gas chambers to kill Jews and giant ovens to burn their bodies. Millions of Jews died in these camps. It was only the military defeat of Germany in World War II that brought an end to the Holocaust. Otherwise, the plan to murder all the Jews of Europe would have been carried through.

The death rate for Jewish children was particularly high during the Holocaust, as many were sent directly to the gas chambers rather than be selected for forced labor. Of the 1.6 million Jewish children in Europe in 1939, more than one million were dead by 1945. Most of those who survived did so by hiding or escaping to safe havens. In this book, we will explore the experiences of children who lived and died during the era of the Holocaust, from the early persecutions to the "final solution."

▲ Children imprisoned at Vittel concentration camp in France stare out from behind a wire fence.

CHAPTER 2

EVERYTHING CHANGES

AS SOON AS THE NAZIS ACHIEVED POWER IN GERMANY IN January 1933, they began to pass measures to restrict the rights of Jews. They banned Jews from working as civil servants, teachers, lawyers, or doctors. Jewish children were prevented from going to school. The so-called Nuremberg Laws of 1935 stripped Jews of their German citizenship and their right to vote, and forbade them from holding public office or from marrying people of "German blood."

▲ Nazi troops stand in front of a Jewish shop in Berlin during a boycott (ban) of Jewish businesses in April 1933. One of the signs says: "Germans defend yourselves! Don't buy from the Jews!"

PREJUDICE

Anti-Semitism (hatred of Jews) was fairly widespread in Europe even before Hitler came to power, and the Nazis were popular among many ordinary Germans.

> 66 When Hitler came to power things changed. We had teachers at school who were very pro-Nazi ... and I was the only Jewish girl in this high school. One particular teacher made my life a misery; she told the girls not to talk to me... And she arranged that I would sit right at the back of the class, two rows were left vacant and I sat against the wall. 99

Ruth Foster, German Jewish schoolgirl, Lingen, age 10 in 1933.

BULLYING

German Jewish children were often picked on by other children, especially by those in the Hitler Youth (a Nazi group for boys and young men). Adults would usually ignore such bullying.

Focus on Ruth Foster

Ruth Foster was born in 1922 in Lingen an der Emms, Germany. In 1941, she was deported to Riga ghetto. After working as a nurse there, she was transported to Stutthof concentration camp. The camp was liberated in 1945. After the war, Ruth married an English doctor, and settled in the U.K.

> 66 After 1933 it was just accepted that if you were a Jewish child you were liable to be beaten up.... It was no use appealing to policemen or teachers because they're not supposed to interfere ... because you are perceived [seen] as an enemy of the state. 99

John Silberman, German Jewish schoolboy, Berlin, age 7 in 1933.

Anti-Semitic graffiti was sprayed on the windows of this Berlin shop in 1938. "Jude" means "Jew." ▶

GROSSE POLITISCHE SCHAU IN DER
NORDWESTBAHNHALLE IN WIEN.
AB 2. AUG. 1938. TÄGLICH GEÖFFNET VON 10-20 UHR

◀ In Nazi Germany, Jews were frequently depicted in cartoons and posters as devious and greedy.

> 66 We used to stand there and read [these newspapers] and look at the pictures [caricatures of Jews]. That was really quite extraordinary, too because we didn't know anyone who looked like that, or had a nose, or ears, or lips like that. I remember reading that Jews also smelled of onions and garlic—I mean we didn't know people like that. 99

Gisela Eisner, German Jewish schoolgirl, Berlin.

PROPAGANDA

Newspapers and books, including children's books, were full of Nazi propaganda – biased information that supported the Nazis. Newspapers often carried anti-Semitic cartoons.

> 66 You opened your first alphabet book, or school book, and the very first picture would be of the Führer ["Leader," meaning Hitler], a very nice Führer, kindly, in civilian clothes.... And the inscription: 'Two things the Führer loves best: children and flowers.' 99

Sergei Hackel, German Jewish schoolboy, Berlin.

GETTING OUT

During the 1930s, many Jewish families decided to leave their homes in Germany to escape the persecution.

> 66 It was pretty early on when those [of our Jewish friends] who could afford to go came to say good-bye. And, of course, those who didn't have the money had to remain. But when they came to say good-bye and said, 'We're going to Shanghai,' 'We're going to America,' 'We're going to...' wherever they managed to go, well, you knew

▲ A Jewish emigration center in Berlin, 1935. Around 38,000 Jews left Germany soon after the Nazi takeover. Most went to neighboring European countries. They were later caught by the Nazis after their conquest of western Europe.

it wasn't because they wanted to go, it was because they were forced to go. **99**

Gerda Williams, German schoolgirl, Berlin.

JUDENREIN

The Nazis passed laws between 1936 and 1939 with the aim of creating a *Judenrein* ("Jewish-cleansed") economy. They set out to "Aryanise" Jewish businesses by dismissing Jewish managers and workers. Nazi officials then sold the Jewish-owned businesses to non-Jewish Germans for bargain prices.

66 *My father's business simply died. Nobody would trade with Jews: you couldn't get supplies, customers, and you couldn't get staff to work for you. If you did you were at their mercy; they could do as they liked—they could steal, they could rob.... A Jew had no rights. I remember that my parents' Gentile [non-Jewish] friends did not stand by them. The average German didn't care: The more Jews that were got rid of, the more of their assets were available to take.* **99**

John Silberman, German Jewish schoolboy, Berlin.

▲ Main image: Cheering crowds line the streets as Nazis drive through Vienna celebrating Germany's takeover of Austria.

Inset, right: Austrian Nazis lead a demonstration in support of the *Anschluss*. ▶

ANSCHLUSS

On March 13, 1938, the Nazis occupied Austria in an event known as the *Anschluss*. Overnight, Austrian Jews lost all their rights and found themselves subjected to violence and humiliation.

66 *I was arrested on Easter Monday, 1938, and taken to the local barracks. I was butted with a rifle and made to lie beneath a mattress on the springs of a bed and four of them jumped on the mattress. I was then taken up to the top floor—by which time they had stripped me to my underpants. They held me out of the window. 'Shall we let him go*

now?' I was sixteen for heaven's sake, not even that! **99**

John Lawrence, Austrian Jewish youth, Vienna, age 16 in 1938.

66 *Within days of Hitler walking in, the janitor in the building where you lived would give you a mop bucket and say, 'Clean the stairs'.... I was amazed that you had no redress [legal rights] against it, but I was told that if you did try and he called in a policeman or Storm Trooper, you could be sent to a concentration camp or they would beat you up and there would be no questions asked.* **99**

Herbert Elliott, Austrian Jewish youth, Vienna.

SUDETENLAND

In September 1938, the Nazis annexed the Sudetenland, an area of Czechoslovakia where many ethnic Germans lived.

66 *After they annexed our part of Czechoslovakia in late 1938, they immediately got rid of our teachers and put in German-trained anti-Semitic Hungarian teachers.... They told the Christian children not to associate with us anymore.... I didn't realize how easy it was to turn somebody's mind, because within days, a friend I used to play with, kick balls with, eat with in each other's houses, all of a sudden called me 'Dirty Jew.'* **99**

Josef Perl, Czech Jewish schoolboy, Velíky Bochkov, age 8 in 1938.

Adolf Hitler is welcomed by crowds lining the streets of Carlsbad in the Sudetenland, Czechoslovakia, following the Nazi takeover. ▼

KRISTALLNACHT

In October 1938, Hitler ordered the expulsion of over 12,000 Polish-born Jews from Germany. Among those expelled were Sendel and Riva Grynszpan. When their son Herschel, who was living in Paris at the time, heard what had happened, he was so angry he assassinated a German diplomat. The Nazis retaliated by launching a series of coordinated attacks on Jews throughout Germany and parts of Austria. *Kristallnacht*, as it became known, took place on the night of November 9–10. By the following morning, at least 91 Jews were dead, and over 7,500 Jewish stores and businesses and 1,000 synagogues were destroyed or damaged.

▲ *Kristallnacht* (Crystal Night) got its name because of all the broken glass that littered the streets after Jewish shops and synagogues had their windows smashed.

> ❝ *A number of men, somewhere between seven and ten, came bursting into our house and started smashing up everything. They locked my parents in the bathroom.... My parents were screaming and shouting because they didn't know what was happening to us, it was really awful.* ❞

Susan Sinclair, German Jewish schoolgirl, Nuremberg, age 15 in 1938.

> ❝ *I stood before the burning shul [synagogue] and watched as the firemen protected the surrounding buildings.... Slowly my senses returned in a wave of anger. I clenched my fists, my eyes filled with tears of outrage.* ❞

Arnold Blum, German Jewish schoolboy, Nuremberg, age 16 in 1938.

As synagogues burned, firefighters were ordered to direct their hoses only on the buildings next to them.

During the *Kristallnacht* riots, these Jewish women in Linz, Austria, were forced to sit in public wearing a sign saying "I have been excluded from the national community." ▶

66 *I saw all these books being burned in the streets and then saw the synagogue on fire. I heard this man calling out and saw that he was being beaten up by these young lads and a couple of men dressed in black uniforms.... I saw that it was my uncle who was being beaten.* 99

John Richards, Austrian Jewish schoolboy, Vienna, age 11 in 1938.

IMPRISONMENT

In the days following *Kristallnacht*, around 30,000 German Jews were arrested and sent to concentration camps. They were released over the next three months, but by then more than 2,000 had died.

66 *After Kristallnacht, my father was imprisoned in Dachau. Eventually, my mother, with a lawyer's help, got him released. He spoke to us about some of his experiences. They were told, 'You can commit suicide if you want—there's the electric fence, but if you attempt it and you don't succeed your punishment will be very heavy.'* 99

Susan Sinclair, German Jewish schoolgirl, Nuremberg, age 15 in 1938.

▲ Some of the young Jewish *Kindertransport* refugees are pictured here on their arrival at Liverpool Street Station in London.

KINDERTRANSPORT

Kristallnacht caused shock and outrage around the world. Within weeks of the event, Britain offered to take in nearly 10,000 Jewish children from Nazi Germany, Austria, and Czechoslovakia. The mission to rescue these children was known as the *Kindertransport* and was organized by charities such as the Red Cross. The children, ages 5 to 17, traveled to Britain without their parents, by train and boat. They were placed in foster homes, hostels, schools, and farms.

66 *I held my sister's hand. We found a compartment. As we got on the train they shut the door, we tried to open the windows and all of a sudden these* black uniforms appeared and they pushed our parents back, they weren't allowed to come near us. Father tried to shout something, but with all the commotion we couldn't hear. The younger children started to cry then… I felt a sense of anger. I thought: was I such a bad lad to be torn away from my father and mother? Will I ever be lucky enough to see them again? 99

John Richards, Austrian Jewish schoolboy, Vienna.

66 *My parents were trying to paint a wonderful picture for me of England: I'm going to a big city, I'm going to school, 'You'll be learning a new language, you'll make new friends, and we'll all be together again soon….* I wanted to believe this but I had all these mixed feelings about it and then I got the notion into my head that my parents wanted to get rid of me. I told them that, and it must have been very painful for them…. 99

Hedy Epstein, German Jewish schoolgirl, Kippenheim.

EMIGRATION

For many Jewish families, *Kristallnacht* was the final straw. In the ten months following *Kristallnacht*, over 115,000 Jews emigrated from Germany. They decided their only hope of survival was to get out of Germany. The majority went to European countries, the United States, Palestine, and Shanghai, China. The Silberman family managed to get a visa to travel to the United States via Britain.

▲ This camp at Dovercourt Bay near Harwich was set up for *Kindertransport* refugees. The camp leader is ringing the dinner bell.

> 66 *I remember standing on the deck watching the German coastline disappear. We arrived in Liverpool the next day. With feelings of renewed hope and great anticipation of the new life which awaited us, we left the ship. As we stepped onto English soil, my father fell to his knees and kissed the ground, shouting in German, 'Gott sei dank, wir sind jetzt frei.' (Thank God, we are now free.)* 99

Marianne Silberman, born Kassel, Germany, 1930.

After World War II began, many territories under Nazi control ordered Jews to wear a yellow Star of David to identify them as Jews. ▶

CHAPTER 3

IN THE GHETTO

IN MARCH 1939, GERMANY COMPLETED ITS OCCUPATION OF Czechoslovakia. The following September, Germany invaded Poland, which prompted Britain and France to declare war on Germany, marking the start of World War II. Shortly after the invasion of Poland, German Nazis began rounding up Polish Jews and sending them to live in enclosed areas of large towns and cities called ghettos. As their territories expanded, the Nazis established ghettos in other eastern European countries and the Soviet Union. The ghettos were surrounded by walls and barbed wire to prevent people from leaving. Any Jew who tried to escape was shot.

LIVING CONDITIONS

Conditions were extremely crowded and unsanitary in the ghettos, with chronic shortages of food. Hundreds of thousands of Jews died of hunger and disease.

▲ Part of the wall enclosing the Jewish ghetto in Warsaw. The ghetto contained over 400,000 Jews in an area of just 1.3 square miles (3.4 square kilometers).

66 *For my brother and me there was no school and the only entertainment was taking a walk. It was unbelievable the number of dead people you saw in the streets. When we came home after a walk it was mandatory [required] that we took off our clothing to search for lice, because they were the ones carrying typhus and typhoid fever.* 99

Jerry Koenig, Polish Jewish child, Warsaw ghetto.

66 *My mother decided that I'm going to have a party.... The birthday party was rather grand because my mother had some oatmeal and she had made some wonderful cookies....*

[The party] was crowned by an incredible thing. I got an orange. I always loved oranges. Only later did I find out that my mother had gone out of the ghetto, sold a diamond and pearl ring to get me an orange. That was the last birthday gift from my parents. **99**

Gerda Weissmann Klein, Polish Jewish child, Bielsko ghetto.

STARVATION RATIONS

Average daily food rations in 1941 for Jews in the Warsaw ghetto were 184 calories, compared to 699 calories for non-Jewish Poles and 2,613 calories for Germans.

66 *Sometimes there was a distribution center and we got a slice of bread and margarine. On occasions we got some cabbage leaves, the outer leaves. In late spring we sometimes got lots of rhubarb leaves and fish heads....*

The food was totally inadequate, especially bearing in mind the cold and people having to work. You'd go out and get weaker and weaker, your movements slower and slower. You'd get starvation signs ... swelling legs, water in the ankles. Then, if you were lucky, pneumonia came and took you away. **99**

Ezra Jurmann, German Jewish child, Riga ghetto.

▲ Jewish children are served a meager meal in the Warsaw ghetto. Many survived only by smuggling in extra food.

▼ Children of the Warsaw ghetto.

Focus on Jerry Koenig

Jerry Koenig was nine when the Germans invaded Poland and he and his family were sent to the Warsaw ghetto. The family escaped and went into hiding on a farm east of Warsaw. In 1944, the family was liberated by the Russian army. Anti-Semitic riots in 1946 forced the Koenigs to flee Poland. They remained in a displaced persons camp until 1951 when they moved to the U.S., settling first in Davenport, Iowa, before moving to St. Louis, Missouri.

▲ Jewish children on a tram in the Warsaw ghetto.

going to be extremely high. So it was no secret in the family that eventually our financial resources would run out and we would face the same situation as the others. **99**

Jerry Koenig, Polish Jewish child, Warsaw ghetto.

EDUCATION

Despite facing terrible hardships, the inhabitants of the ghettos tried to continue children's education by setting up secret schools.

GROWING UP FAST

Children often had to care for younger siblings after the death or deportation of their parents. Many became smugglers, helping to save people from starvation. In the Warsaw ghetto, hundreds of four- to eight-year-old Jewish children sneaked over to the "Aryan side" several times a day, returning with food and other essentials.

66 *The only way you could survive was by supplementing your diet with things bought through the black market. But you can imagine that if the sellers were risking their lives to obtain these things, then the price is*

66 *Schools were forbidden, but parents organized small groups of children, four or five at a time. We met once or twice a week in somebody's room, usually in a different room every*

A secret network of religious schools was set up for both boys and girls in the Warsaw ghetto. ▼

▲ The Nazis often used terror tactics to keep order in the ghettos. Here, the Gestapo (Nazi secret police) launch a raid on the Warsaw ghetto.

week because there was the death penalty for the children, the teachers, the parents, and in fact everybody in the house if we were discovered. We had classes in just the basics, we couldn't learn physics or chemistry properly as we couldn't have laboratories or make experiments; we learned all that from books, which were ... out of date, but we learned with great enthusiasm. 99

Janina David, Polish Jewish child, Warsaw ghetto.

66 *In the very beginning, my mother and several other women organized a clandestine school for children.... [They] would barter on the outside*

and they came home with crayons, with writing paper, with some books, and ... they would tell stories, we would sing and we would color, and it was something to look forward to... if it only could have lasted, but it didn't. It lasted a few months. And pretty soon there was not enough jewelry or money to barter with. There were no more supplies ... and the morale sort of sagged in the ghetto. 99

Charlene Schiff, Polish Jewish child, Horochow ghetto.

JUDENRAT

The Nazis appointed councils of Jews, called *Judenrat*, to run the ghettos. The *Judenrat* helped ease suffering in the ghettos. They set up soup kitchens, orphanages, and hospitals. They also helped distribute food and medical aid, but they were essentially puppets of the Nazis. There was also a Jewish police force in the ghetto responsible for keeping order.

66 *I went stealing bread with the orphans. I wanted to be one of the boys. I was a thin little boy, so they had me one time climb up … a rain drainpipe … to the first floor … they had a warehouse there for bread.… I started throwing down bread to them and then the Jewish police … caught me.… The bigger children ran away … but me they caught and they caught three or four more. And they took us to the 'Kommissariat' … and the person in charge … the 'Yiddishe Politzei' [Jewish policeman], he decided to give us … ten whips with a rubber hose.* **99**

Yaacov Schwartzberger, Lithuanian Jewish child, Vilna ghetto.

PLAYTIME

Most children in the ghettos didn't have toys. They were forced to find different ways to entertain themselves and forget their miseries for a while, using fantasy, creativity, and play.

66 *…I remember making little dolls out of curtain rings and playing with those.* **99**

Alice Meroudas, Polish Jewish child, Lvov ghetto.

Deprived of toys and playthings in the ghetto, children were forced to find other ways to entertain themselves. ▲

▲ These Jewish children have been forced to clean the street in their Polish ghetto.

DEPORTATIONS

In 1942, the Nazis began Operation Reinhard, deporting Jews from the ghettos with the aim of closing the ghettos down. The Nazis called it "resettlement," but in fact they were sending the Jews to slave-labor and death camps. Many of those first selected for deportation were children and old people.

66 ...There were a lot of children my own age ... and we used to gather in the attic sort of place, sing songs and make up plays, and talk, and played games, you know, all kinds of games and amused ourselves.... In the spring then we used to go for walks; there was a place ... it was in the boundary of the ghetto, but it was like a sort of wasteground, there weren't any houses, and occasionally there was a tree, because I remember trying to eat the bark of it, to see if one could eat it, which you couldn't.... 99

Edith Birkin, Czech Jewish child, Lodz ghetto.

66 At one stage the SS [the Nazi force mainly responsible for carrying out the Holocaust] came along and told Rumkowski [leader of the Judenrat] that he had to supply so many children. And Rumkowski called a meeting that we had to attend. He stood up in Lodz Square and said, 'I appeal to you to give up your children. We have this demand; in order for you to survive, your children must be given up.' He stood there and uttered those words. I found that speech of Rumkowski's terrible. At a certain point you have to say, 'No, I will not do this, I will not say this.' 99

Roman Halter, Polish Jewish youth, Lodz ghetto.

ROUNDING UP CHILDREN

❝ *The children … tried to run back to their mothers….And babies, little children, lovely children. The guards looked everywhere: they opened every cellar and just pulled them out like catching rabbits, and from attics, from gardens, from everywhere. Mothers tried to give them wedding rings, everything they had. To describe how the children were herded to these lorries is impossible.* ❞

Marsha Segall, young Lithuanian woman, Siauliai ghetto.

▲ Jews from the Warsaw ghetto are lined up by German soldiers prior to deportation.

SELECTING WHO SHOULD LIVE

Ryvka "Rene" Salt was a Polish Jewish child at Zdunska Wola ghetto. In August 1942 her family were woken up by the shout, "All Jews out! Into the streets!" They went out and were led to a big field where they were ordered to sit down. Parents were told to give up any child under the age of eighteen.

66 *When they had taken all the children, we were lined up in fives and taken to the local [Jewish] cemetery where there was a selection: right to live, left to be taken away.... I was spotted by a German officer.... 'You, stand up! How old are you?' I was so nervous, I couldn't answer. My father said, 'Oh, she's eighteen, I know her.'*

The officer stood there looking at me—I was twelve and looked about eight—he ... could see that I wasn't eighteen years old. Finally, he said, 'She can sit down.' No one could believe it.... When we left that cemetery, there were only three children left, I was one of the three. 99

September 1942: children from Lodz ghetto in Poland are about to be deported to Chelmno extermination camp.

▲ A building burns during the Warsaw ghetto uprising. The uprising took place during April and May 1943. Around 13,000 Jews were killed. The German death toll is unknown.

HIDING PLACE

In July 1942, when the large-scale deportations started, the Nazis would often catch people as they were running back home after work. Edyta Klein-Smith was a child in the Warsaw ghetto at the time. She and her stepfather were running home when they saw the soldiers and they knew they weren't going to make it to their house. Then her stepfather remembered that someone had built a hiding place behind a wall in a nearby building. They ran to the building.

66 *This hiding place was very small and it was packed, but our relatives were there and they let us in. The wall was closed so completely on the outside that you couldn't see anything. The Germans came running through the building shooting and pounding on the doors.* 99

Edyta Klein-Smith, Polish Jewish child, Warsaw ghetto.

WARSAW GHETTO UPRISING

By 1943, many Jews in the ghettos had learned the truth about where the Nazis were sending them, and Jewish resistance groups began ghetto uprisings. The biggest of these happened at the Warsaw ghetto. Children fought alongside adults, using pistols and petrol bombs against Nazi tanks and machine guns. All the uprisings failed.

> *I was there at the time of the uprising and I have seen young boys and girls running around in the middle of the night across roofs, through sewers…. By then there was a shortage of people in the ghetto so there was furniture and things to barter, not for food, but for arms…. I remember seeing boys and girls, who were no older than seventeen or eighteen, going to kill Germans and taking their machine guns away. They said: 'we don't mind giving our lives so long as some can save themselves.'*

Stanley Faull, Polish Jewish child, Warsaw ghetto.

Jews captured during the Warsaw ghetto uprising. Of the 50,000 Jews who survived the German counterattack, most were captured and sent to concentration and death camps. ▼

CHAPTER 4

I▮TO HIDING

MOST OF THE CHILDREN WHO SURVIVED THE HOLOCAUST DID so by going into hiding. To escape roundups, deportations, and death, children hid in sewers, barns, rivers, cupboards, and attics. Some took on false identities, posing as non-Jews. Others stayed concealed from the outside world for weeks or even years. They lived constantly with the fear of discovery, betrayal, and death.

FLEEING THE GHETTO

66 *Mother and I fled... We hid, submerged in the water, all night as machine guns blazed in the ghetto. By morning others were hiding in the brush and I heard a Ukrainian guard scream, 'I see you there Jews; come out!' Most obeyed, but we stayed in the water for several more days... Once I woke to find Mother had vanished.* 99

Charlene Schiff, Polish Jewish child, age 13 when she went into hiding

HIDDEN IN A SUITCASE

During a roundup of children at the Kovno ghetto in Lithuania, 14-year-old David Levine had to think very quickly when he heard soldiers

◀ A Lithuanian Nazi policeman rounding up Jews in the Vilna ghetto.

coming. They wouldn't take him—he was old enough to work—but where could he hide his two-year-old nephew?

> " *I pulled a suitcase out from under my bed and I put [my nephew] in the suitcase and I told him, 'You may not cry, you may not speak, and you may not say anything or shout because if you do,' I said, 'the Germans will take you and you will die.' He understood… Within a minute, a Ukrainian soldier came through the door of the apartment, and he asked were there any children here. And I said, 'No there aren't any.'…And he looked and looked. Of course, he didn't find. The little boy didn't say anything.* "

▲ Krystyna Chiger (left) pictured before the war with her brother Pawelek and their parents. In the sewer they had to get used to huge rats, flooding, and terrible cold.

LIVING IN THE SEWERS

In 1943 as the Germans arrived to close down the Lvov ghetto, seven-year-old Krystyna Chiger and her family fled to the sewers.

> " *Some people couldn't take the stench and the darkness, so they left, but ten of us remained in that sewer—for fourteen months! … we never went outside or saw daylight.*

> *We lived with webs and moss hanging on the wall. The river not only smelled terrible, but also it was full of diseases. We got dysentery… There was only enough clean water for each of us to have half a cup a day… The rats were all over us… nobody had to tell us to be quiet. I felt like an animal, ruled by instinct.* "

Focus on Charlene Schiff

Charlene Schiff was born in 1929 in Horochow, Poland. In 1941, her father was arrested and never heard from again. She, her mother, and her sister were forced into Horochow ghetto.

When they escaped in 1942, her sister got separated and was presumably caught and killed. Charlene and her mother hid for several days in underbrush at the edge of a river. One morning she awoke to find her mother had disappeared. Charlene survived by herself in the forests until liberated by Soviet troops. She eventually emigrated to the United States.

▲ This photo shows Charlene Schiff in 1945. She survived the war to build a new life in the United States, but none of her family survived.

HIDDEN AWAY

Going into hiding usually meant relying on other people for shelter, food, and news. Parents made preparations in advance and rarely told their children what they were planning. Some non-Jewish people offered to hide Jewish children for free; others needed to be paid. Hidden away in apartments and special hiding places, children stayed silent and never went out.

66 *The plan was to dig a shelter inside of a barn.... The shelter was to be big enough to house eleven people....*

All the digging had to be done at night and carried to the fields by hand.... The walls of the shelter were lined with straw, there were branches on the floor to keep water from coming up, and there was a trap door, which, when lifted up, was still inside the barn. We actually went into the shelter in the winter of 1942–1943 and stayed there twenty months until liberation came. 99

Jerry Koenig, Polish Jewish child, Kosow.

◀ Otto Wolf and his sister Felicitas shown with Otto's diary. Felicitas continued the diary after Otto was captured in 1945.

September 19, 1942 We are depressed, wondering how things will go. Who will give us sanctuary...?

March 14, 1945 There is a lot of snow in the forest. We cut armfuls of small branches. We can't walk around there. It is really miserable in the forest now. **99**

Otto Wolf, Czech teenager.

IN THE WOODS

Otto Wolf was 15 years old when his family escaped deportation by hiding in woods around Mohelnice, Czechoslovakia. Otto kept a diary. In 1945, just weeks before the end of the war, he was captured and shot.

66 *August 25, 1942 In the afternoon something scares us terribly. We hear a noise in the hut. We were really scared.*

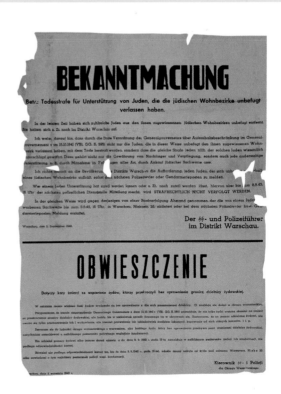

This German poster of September 1942 warns that helping Jews from the Warsaw ghetto is punishable by death. ▶

ANNE FRANK'S DIARY

Anne Frank was a German Jewish girl. She and her family moved to Amsterdam in 1933 to escape persecution by the Nazis. When the Nazis invaded the Netherlands, the Franks were forced to go into hiding in a secret annex at the back of her father Otto's office building. For two years they and a few others remained hidden, unable to venture outside or make any noise.

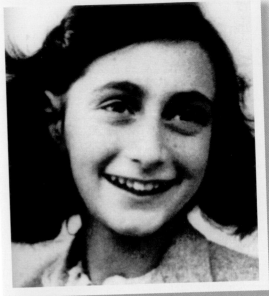

Anne decided to keep a diary recording her thoughts and feelings. In the summer of 1944, they were betrayed.

Anne, her sister, and her mother were sent to the camps where they died. Anne's father survived, and after the war, he published Anne's diary as a book. It went on to become an international best seller and one of the most famous books of the 20th century.

◀ A large, false bookcase concealed the entrance to the secret annex where Anne Frank and her family hid in Amsterdam.

CABINET

“ *My father had gold coins, and with that he was able to buy us shelter on a farm…. we stayed in what was actually a cabinet, only about sixty or seventy centimeters wide. The length of it would have been a couple of meters, because we could all lie on top of each other comfortably…. This cabinet was in a cellar, so it was well hidden. Our presence there was so secret, not even the children of the hiding family knew we were there. That was where we stayed for thirteen months!* ”

Richard Rozen, Polish Jewish boy, age 6 when he went into hiding.

Children who went into hiding often had to conceal themselves in wardrobes or other hiding places every time there was a knock on the door. ▼

RABBITS

Alicia Adams, a Jewish child from Drobhobycz in Poland, came close to being killed by the German man who was hiding her.

“ *He was charging so much per head for every Jew and he hid us in his cellar where he had another fifteen already hidden. He called us his 'rabbits' and in the evening he would call his 'rabbits' out and give us some food. … One night we heard him talking with his wife. She said, 'How are you going to kill them?' And he said, 'Well, I kill animals all the time—a sheep, a cow—it can't be so different to kill a man.' But somehow he was afraid to do it and we were lucky.* ”

HIDING IN THE OPEN

One way of hiding was to pretend not to be a Jew. This meant living openly but as a Christian. Jewish children who had so-called "Aryan" features, such as blond hair and blue eyes, could more easily disguise themselves, but even children with more Jewish features used false identities. Living under a false identity put great strain on children. Many had to leave parents behind.

66 *... Fourteen thousand Jews were arrested in a roundup. A secret maid's room was found for my parents to hide in. My two sisters and I were sent off to a convent called 'La Chaumiere' [The Cottage] in Flers in Normandy. I really felt abandoned but I couldn't say so. Ours was not the usual kind of hiding. We were not in an attic or underground. We were in plain sight. What we* were hiding was our Jewishness. We no longer wore the Star of David. We were passing for Catholics. 99

Renee Roth-Hano, German Jewish schoolgirl, age 11 when she went into hiding.

66 *Marysia [aunt's maid] ... took us to Otyniowicy, a village in the Ukraine, where her sister lived. The village was very primitive, and Marysia's sister, Nascia Puchal and her daughter,*

Renee Roth-Hano (standing on the right) pictured in 1944 with her sisters and two of the nuns who sheltered them in Normandy. ▶

Marynka, were the poorest family…. Nascia never knew we were Jewish. She just needed help making a living…. Nascia's brother was a gravedigger and very anti-Semitic…. We had to live and behave as Christians. I was expected to go to confession. I didn't have the slightest idea what to do….

I'd made friends with some Ukrainian children and I said to one girl, 'Tell me how to go to confession in Ukrainian and I'll tell you how to do it in Polish.' … I got away with that. **99**

Rosa Sirota, Polish Jewish girl, age 8 when she went into hiding.

Focus on Nelly Toll

When Nelly Toll was eight, she and her mother went into hiding with a Christian Polish couple. Nelly later spoke of her experience: "Sometimes I wondered if I would ever be able to go out again, to walk and run as the kids outside did. At those times it seemed as if I would be in this room forever."

◀ ▲ Nelly was given some paints, and to escape the tedium of the days, she painted happy scenes such as these.

▲ Pre-war photo of Sabina (right) and Helka Zimering and their parents. After the war, Zimering repaid the kindness of her Catholic friends in Poland by testifying to their heroism.

A NARROW ESCAPE

With the help of close Catholic friends, Sabina Zimering and her sister Helka escaped from the ghetto in her Polish town hours before they would have been deported to Treblinka. Her friends got them false identification papers and

◄ Forged identity papers such as this were vital to Jewish children trying to pass as Christians.

they went to Germany posing as Polish Catholic workers. They found work in a fancy hotel where all the guests were German officers and members of the Gestapo (Nazi secret police).

> 66 *Helka and I realized that we lived and worked in the midst of our most powerful and feared enemies.... They assumed I was one of the Christian foreign workers helping in the war effort.... I was vacuuming the large, beautiful ballroom ... an officer motioned me to stop the noise. With a curious look, he asked me where I was from. 'I have watched you work,' he said,* 'and noticed the shape of your head, your profile, and ears. I am an anthropologist with a special interest in the Jewish facial structure. Are there any Jews in your family?' Panic filled me instantly.... I said, 'Jews in my family? Never. We never had any. What nonsense.' Without looking at him, I turned on the loud vacuum cleaner and continued to work.* 99

Sabina Zimering, Polish Jewish teenager.

▲ Rosary beads given to Lida Kleinman who hid in Catholic orphanages in Poland during the war.

DISGUISED AS A GIRL

Because all Jewish boys are circumcised, it was much harder for boys to pretend to be Gentiles. Taking off their pants would reveal the truth.

> 66 *My fictional name was Marysia Ulecki. I was supposed to be a distant cousin of the people who were keeping my mother and me. The physical part was easy. After a couple of years in hiding with no haircuts, my hair was very long. The big problem was language. My mother spent a lot of time teaching me to speak and walk and act like a girl.* 99

Richard Rozen, Polish Jewish boy.

▲ Lida Kleinman as a child in the 1930s. Lida, her father, and some family members survived the war, but her mother did not.

◀ This group photograph shows Lida Kleinman with her face scratched out.

The need for security

Children pretending to be Gentiles (non-Jews) had to remember never to reveal their Jewishness. From 1942 Lida Kleinman, the daughter of well-to-do Polish parents, lived in Catholic convents. She was so anxious that when a group photograph was taken, she scratched out her face because she thought it looked "too Jewish."

A DOUBLE LIFE

66 *At night I covered my head with the blanket and cried. After only a month of hiding I wished I could turn the clock back and be in the warmth of my beloved family. It was not easy for me to live a double life, pretend to be Borishka, a good Catholic girl, when inside me I was still the Jewish Hedi.* 99

Hedi Fischer Frankl, Hungarian Jewish girl, age 14 when she went into hiding.

EXPOSED

Hedi Fischer Frankl, a 14-year-old Hungarian Jewish girl, took the identity of a Catholic girl, Borishka Kovacs. Feeling lonely and homesick, she befriended two other Jewish girls also living under false papers. Later, her friends' real identities were exposed. Their landlady told the police that a slim, dark-haired girl named Borishka often visited.

66 *[The police] proceeded to torture and threatened to kill the girls unless they revealed who and where Borishka was. At 3 A.M. the girls led the detectives to where I lived. Suddenly, there was a loud banging on our windows: 'Open up, Police!' they bellowed.... The detectives entered my bedroom. 'Get up, get dressed, you are coming with us,' they urged me.... 'I am a good practicing Christian....' I pleaded. 'You are Hedi Fischer, and don't try to fool us. We know that you are Jewish.'* 99

Hedi was sent to a concentration camp in Austria, but managed to survive the war.

This well-worn teddy bear was owned by Fred Lessing, a Jewish child who posed as a Christian for two and a half years. He later said: "My little Bear—he never had a name—went with me everywhere. He kept me company and he kept my secret." ▼

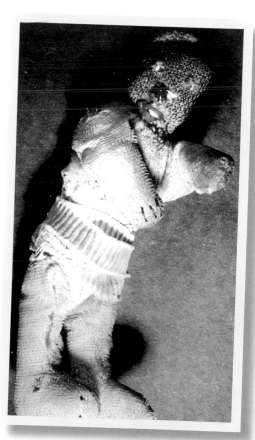

Jewish children pictured at Le Chambon-sur-Lignon in front of the building where they were given shelter by the local Protestant population. ▼

Partisans

Another way in which Jewish children hid was by joining the partisans—secret groups that existed throughout occupied Europe dedicated to attacking the Nazis. Daniel "Danko" Ivin was a ten-year-old Jewish child, who joined a partisan unit in Croatia. He recalls some of the hard times they went through.

❝ Autumn of '42 we were in the woods ... without water and salt. You had rotten trees falling down and when it rained they were full of water and if you squeezed this wood then a few drops, very bitter and brownish, came out; that is all we had for about ten to fifteen days, and it was terrible for the wounded. We were also without food, we were cooking grass that you find in the woods, no salt—so very hungry and without water then. ❞

LE CHAMBON-SUR-LIGNON

People who hid Jewish children and helped them to survive the Holocaust took terrible risks. Children were hidden in Catholic convents and religious orphanages. Underground networks and partisans also helped to smuggle children to safe hideouts. In southern France hundreds of Jewish children were sheltered by people in the village of Le Chambon-sur-Lignon. Villagers, led by Protestant pastor Andre Trocmé, organized false papers and ration books and hid children in their homes, schools, and on farms. To hide their Jewish identity, children often attended Christian church services.

> 66 *They just accepted us, taking us in with warmth, sheltering children, often without their parents—children who cried in the night from nightmares.* 99

Elizabeth Koenig-Kaufman, child refugee.

Some of the Jewish refugees at Le Chambon-sur-Lignon, photographed in 1941. ▼

CHAPTER 5

CAMPS

THE NAZIS CREATED A NETWORK OF CONCENTRATION CAMPS IN the territories they occupied. Millions of prisoners, including Jews, were sent there to be used for slave labor. Conditions were appalling, and huge numbers died of starvation, exhaustion, and abuse. There were also extermination camps—killing centers—where an estimated 3.5 million Jews died.

▲ A train full of Jewish prisoners arrives at a concentration camp.

> **We were like sardines. In one corner a young couple were sitting with a baby, warming some milk or water with a candle to give the baby something to drink. The stench in that train! I cannot tell you.... We were like animals.**

Barbara Stimler, Polish Jewish girl, Auschwitz-Birkenau.

> **We were loaded into cattle trucks, which were then sealed. The temperature in the Hungarian summer was nearly 100 degrees [Fahrenheit] and we were given no water or bread, only a bucket to be used as a toilet. Soldiers with dogs and bayonets were guarding us all the way on a horrific journey that lasted five days and nights....There were 80 people, old and young, some sick, but**

TRAIN JOURNEY

Jews were transported to the camps by train on closed, overcrowded freight or cattle wagons, often without food, water, ventilation, or toilets. Many died on these journeys.

none of us had enough space to lie down. The constant heat, hunger, thirst, and lack of sleep made us quite delirious. 🙶

Hedi Fischer Frankl, Hungarian Jewish girl, age 14.

ARRIVAL

Upon reaching a camp, men and women were separated. The children stayed with their mothers. Prisoners were ordered to undress and have their hair shaved off before showering. Clothing was replaced by a striped uniform. Each prisoner was given a number, which was tattooed on their arm.

🙶 *We were told to take our clothes off, they stripped us…. Here in my ear is this big hole—they couldn't take my*

▲ A woman and some children, newly arrived at Auschwitz-Birkenau, who have been selected for the gas chamber.

earring out quickly enough. After this, the showers; then we had to stand naked with arms up in the air, and they shaved you everywhere…. I was calling my mother. I hardly recognized her, nor her me because we had no hair; and I had a head of lovely red hair! 🙶

Helen Pelc, Polish Jewish girl, Auschwitz-Birkenau.

JUST A NUMBER

🙶 *The next part was getting my number tattooed…. in Auschwitz you became a number, you didn't know anybody.* 🙶

Jan Hartman, Czech Jewish boy, Auschwitz-Birkenau.

▲ The entrance to Auschwitz concentration camp. The words above the gate are "*Arbeit macht frei*" (Work makes you free).

Focus on Roman Halter

Roman Halter was born in 1927 in Chodecz, Poland, the youngest of seven children. He spent the war in Lodz ghetto, and Auschwitz-Birkenau and Stuthoff concentration camps, before being used as a slave laborer in a Dresden factory. In 1945, Roman came to Britain as one of "the Boys" (see pages 42–43) and became an architect. In 1974 he began recording his Holocaust experiences in paintings and stained-glass windows.

> **"** *I worked in Buna where the I G Farben industry was located.... The firm had to pay the SS for each slave laborer and naturally they only wanted people who could work. They worked them to death because how long could you labor with just the little bit of food we were given!* **"**

John Fink, Germany Jewish youth, Auschwitz-Birkenau.

> **"** *There was this big trough of disinfectant, which looked like iodine, and we had to submerge ourselves in that. If we didn't submerge fully, a SS would stand on you with their boots until even our heads were submerged. With the rough shaving we'd had, anyone who was cut suffered tremendously because it stung so badly.* **"**

Roman Halter, Polish Jewish boy, Auschwitz-Birkenau.

FACTORY WORK

The inmates of concentration camps were forced to work as slave laborers in nearby factories. When they were no longer strong enough to work, they were killed.

Senior Nazi officials inspect one of the factories at Auschwitz-Birkenau. The life expectancy of Jews working in these factories was three to four months. ▼

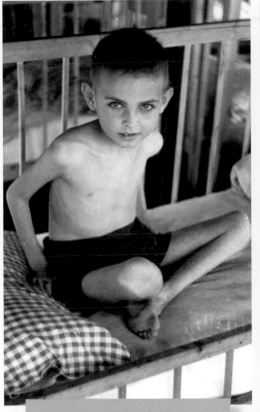

▲ A child at Bergen-Belsen concentration camp after the camp was liberated by British troops in 1945. Around 700 children were found, many close to starvation.

66 *We arrived and were sent to Work C, which was an ammunition factory.... Most of the time I worked on boring holes in shells. TNT, a yellow stuff, which looks like semolina when it's dry, was melted in big boilers, then ... poured into shells.... The dust would come out on your face, and ate into your lungs, and you became yellow with it. We worked on twelve-hour shifts. Work C was the worst place, the survival rate was very poor and thousands died there.* 99

Alfred Huberman, Polish Jewish youth, Skarzysko-Kamienna.

STARVATION RATIONS

Breakfast in the camps would be imitation coffee or herbal tea. For lunch, prisoners were given watery soup. In the evening they received a small piece of black bread and occasionally a tiny piece of sausage, marmalade, or cheese. These rations were intended only to keep prisoners alive. Many thousands died from starvation or diseases caused by malnutrition.

66 *Our barracks were bare; our bed had only straw on it and was full of bedbugs.... We had to walk 5 km [3 miles] to our work place and lived on black coffee, a small piece of bread, and a kind of soup. Needless to say, we were very hungry all the time and could not think of anything else except of getting hold of some real food.* 99

Hedi Fischer Frankl, Hungarian Jewish schoolgirl, Strasshof.

> ❝ …We were eating grass—clover and shamrock…. I would … draw a plate of food and someone would say, 'Oh, can you draw nice sliced bread?' They were going crazy for food. It was always in your mind. Or an apple, I would draw that if they wanted. ❞

Clare Parker, Hungarian Jewish girl, Mauthausen.

HIDDEN CHILDREN

At Plaszow concentration camp, some mothers drugged their children with sleep medications and smuggled them into their barracks. It didn't take the authorities long to find the children.

> ❝ The Germans got to know about the children hidden in our barrack. They handled it in a very nice way: a nursery would be arranged for when the women were working…. Suddenly we saw a lorry with all the children on it; next to me stood a mother with twins of eleven, and those poor girls were crying, 'Mother, mother! They're taking us away.' And they did, the children disappeared. ❞

Taube Biber, Polish Jewish girl, Plaszow.

KINDERLAGER

The children selected for slave labor at Auschwitz-Birkenau were housed in a "children's camp," or *Kinderlager*. They were treated much like the adults, and lived with constant hunger, fear, and exhaustion. Most of the inmates in the Kinderlager were teenagers. A few were younger. The youngest and smallest of all may have been Tova Friedman (née Tola Grossman), who was not yet six when she arrived at the camp.

> ❝ … A woman came to the Kinderlager and handed me a cloth bag that was sewn shut. When I opened the bag I found a piece of bread wrapped in a note: 'Tola,' it said, 'tomorrow is your birthday. I love you. Mama.'

Children at Auschwitz-Birkenau. Around 232,000 children were deported to the camp, and some 700 remained alive at liberation. ▼

That night I hid the treasured food under my dress. I would eat it the next day, on my birthday. In the middle of the night, I woke up to the sound of squeaks. Rats were crawling all over me. Terrified, I lay frozen until they finished nibbling the bread. After they crawled away, I looked at my dress; it was torn. But my visitors left me without a scratch ... or a spare crumb. **99**

Tova Friedman, Jewish girl.

DEATH CAMPS

From December 1941, the first of six extermination camps began operating. The majority of Holocaust victims were murdered at these camps. They were poisoned in gas chambers disguised as shower units, and their bodies were burned in giant ovens.

Auschwitz-Birkenau was a concentration camp as well as an extermination camp. As each trainload of Jews arrived, a Nazi doctor would choose who was fit enough for work and who should die. Babies and young children were almost always sent directly to the gas chamber. Teenagers had a better chance of survival, particularly if they said they had a skill.

MENGELE

Josef Mengele was a German SS officer and doctor who carried out "medical experiments" on hundreds of children in the *Kinderlager* at Auschwitz-Birkenau. For example, he would carry out surgical operations on them, removing organs without anesthetic.

66 *Every day, children were taken for Dr. Mengele's experiments. Some of the children would come back to the barracks, covered with bandages and curled up in pain. Others woudn't come back at all.* **99**

Frieda Tennenbaum, Polish Jewish girl, born 1934.

A gas chamber at Auschwitz-Birkenau. It now contains a candle-lit shrine to commemorate all who died in there. ▼

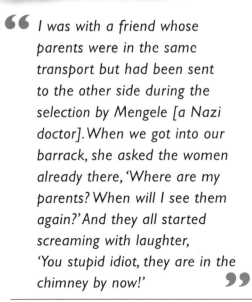

▲ The interior of a crematorium at Auschwitz-Birkenau. At the height of the killings, the crematoria were burning thousands of corpses a day.

❝ *I was with a friend whose parents were in the same transport but had been sent to the other side during the selection by Mengele [a Nazi doctor]. When we got into our barrack, she asked the women already there, 'Where are my parents? When will I see them again?' And they all started screaming with laughter, 'You stupid idiot, they are in the chimney by now!'* ❞

Anna Bergman, Czech Jewish girl, Auschwitz-Birkenau.

WARNINGS

Helga Weiss was 14 when she was sent to Auschwitz-Birkenau. She remembered the whispered warnings when she arrived: "Don't say you are too young, don't say you are ill—say you are able to work." Luckily, the SS man didn't ask questions, and both her and her mother were selected to live. The next day, a Nazi officer addressed the women:

> **The speech was very long—I asked my mother to translate. She said, 'Oh, he says we are in an extermination camp'…. We arrived and saw smoking chimneys—we thought it was a factory.**

LIVING IN THE MIDST OF DEATH

> **What struck me about the camp was the smell. By then we knew it was an extermination camp…. 'You go through the chimney'—that was the standard saying. I never heard about the gas chambers, so I didn't know how people were killed. But we saw the chimneys and we associated the flames with the transports coming in … there was the smell of human flesh being burnt, a certain smell, it was the air … you were breathing the dead.**

Jan Hartman, Czech Jewish youth, Auschwitz-Birkenau.

Marion Blumenthal Lazan, a young inmate at Bergen-Belsen concentration camp, recalls the day she saw a wagon passing by her barracks. At first she thought it was carrying wood.

> **I soon realized they were dead bodies, piled one on top of the other and I was only nine years old.**

THE *SONDERKOMMANDO*

The bodies of gas chamber victims were disposed of by Jews called *Sonderkommandos*. They were forced to do this work, and could only avoid it by committing suicide. Fifteen-year-old Henry Sperling, a Polish Jew, was one of those selected for this gruesome duty. He wrote:

▲ A collage by a child inmate of Terezín concentration camp. About 15,000 children passed through Terezín, most of whom went on to die at Auschwitz. They are chiefly remembered by the drawings and poems they made at Terezín.

> " *Death is constantly before our eyes. New transports arrive all the time. On average, 10,000 people per day are murdered. There was one day when the human transport reached 24,000.* "

STAY FIT OR DIE

Majdanek, like Auschwitz-Birkenau, was both a concentration camp and an extermination camp.

> " *If you became ill, the 'hospital' was really a staging area for the gas chamber, as there were*

> *no doctors or nurses and very little medicine. So one had to keep fit in order to survive.* "

Stanley Faull, Polish Jewish youth, Majdanek.

> " *The Sonderkommando foreman told me, 'We have to empty the gas chamber by loading the bodies onto trolleys ... then take them by rail to the crematorium where they are burnt.* "

Michael Honey, Czech Jewish youth, Auschwitz-Birkenau.

The entrance to Auschwitz-Birkenau death camp as it appears today. ▼

CHAPTER 6

LIBERATION AND AFTERMATH

BY THE SUMMER AND AUTUMN OF 1944, THE GERMAN ARMY WAS in retreat. The Soviet Union's "Red Army" was pushing through Poland in the east, while British and American forces were liberating large parts of western Europe. As the Red Army approached the concentration and extermination camps of eastern Europe, the Nazis tried to make sure that no evidence remained of their cruelty and mass murder.

DEATH MARCHES

Before the Soviet forces arrived, the Nazi authorities ordered the evacuation of the camps. At first, most of the prisoners were sent on trains west toward Germany. As winter approached, the German railways came under Allied bombardment, and the Nazi authorities began evacuating the camps on foot. Prisoners, including children, were led west on what became known as "death marches." Many froze to death, starved or were shot during the journey.

> 66 *One night it must have been thirty-five degrees below zero … we all had completely white noses like pieces of ice, completely frozen. And we learned something that I didn't know was possible—you could walk and sleep at the same time. So we devised a way that the five of us were supporting*

35.000 HÄFTLINGE WERDEN AUF DEN TODESMARSCH GETRIEBEN, 21. APRIL BIS 9. MAI 1945

◀ This display panel from a Holocaust museum in Germany shows a photograph of the death march from Sachsenhausen concentration camp, during which thousands died.

the girl in the middle who was hanging on asleep and the feet and legs were still moving. **99**

Zdenka Ehrlich, Czech Jewish girl, Kurzbach to Bergen-Belsen march.

FROZEN TO DEATH

For parts of the journey, prisoners were put on open railway carriages. It was a very harsh winter, and many died from the cold.

66 *I just remember waking up on a layer of dead people, frozen like stone—many layers of them, three, four, five layers high.* **99**

Jan Hartman, Czech Jewish boy, Czechowice to Buchenwald march.

SHOOTING PRISONERS

The SS guards were instructed to kill prisoners who could no longer walk, or keep pace with the rest.

66 *We were marching five abreast. At the end of each group were those who couldn't walk and they were shot; the result was that when we got to Mauthausen we were only three thousand out of the ten thousand who had started off.* **99**

Harry Lowit, Czech Jewish boy, Auschwitz to Ebensee march.

LIBERATION

The Soviet Red Army entered the first of the camps, Majdanek, in July 1944. The Nazis tried to destroy evidence of their crimes before they fled, yet Soviet forces found gas chambers, remains of crematoria, and warehouses full of prisoners' belongings. They also found tens of thousands of prisoners, many of them close to death. During the autumn and winter, more camps were overrun, and further evidence of Nazi atrocities came to light. British and American forces liberated the concentration camps of Buchenwald, Dachau, Mauthausen, and Bergen-Belsen in April 1945.

Young prisoners at Dachau concentration camp cheer U.S. troops who have arrived to liberate the camp. ▼

◀ A young survivor of Bergen-Belsen manages a smile following the liberation of the camp by British forces.

66 *When they started feeding us, my first meal consisted of a quarter of a slice of white bread topped with a teaspoonful of stewed apples. The taste is still in my mouth today. I shall never forget that meal, never!* 99

Ryvka "Rene" Salt, Polish Jewish child, Bergen-Belsen.

BYSTANDERS

A great many ordinary people in Germany and occupied Europe knew about what was happening to the Jews, but did nothing about it. Why was this? Some may have been anti-Semitic themselves. Others may have been too scared to help because they were afraid of getting punished. Most probably

turned a blind eye because it was easier, in the end, to ignore something that didn't affect them personally.

On the death march from Neustadt to Bergen-Belsen, Olga Albogen mentions how when they passed through a village, they were ignored:

66 *… We saw them—from the curtains they were peeking out and watching and looking, but nobody came near us.…* 99

CHILDREN AT AUSCHWITZ

The Red Army liberated Auschwitz-Birkenau in January 1945. Among the surviving prisoners were several hundred children, including 10-year-old twin sisters Eva and Miriam Mozes. They had survived despite being subjected to Dr. Mengele's experiments. Eva remembers the moment the Soviet soldiers entered the camp.

> 66 *We ran up to them and they gave us hugs, cookies, and chocolate. Being so alone, a hug meant more than anybody could imagine.... We were not only starved for food but we were starved for human kindness. And the Soviet Army did provide some of that.* 99

Eva Mozes, Romanian Jewish girl, age 10 in 1945.

DISPLACED CHILDREN

The Holocaust left huge numbers of Jewish refugees homeless and separated from their families. Among the refugees were thousands of children. Most were placed in displaced persons (DP) camps under the control of Allied forces. Great efforts were made to reunite children with surviving members of their family. Not all family reunions were happy. After years of separation, some children barely remembered their parents or relatives. And not all family members were sympathetic to their suffering.

> 66 *And [my uncle] said, 'Just remember, in my house I do not wish to hear one word of what happened to you during the war. I don't want to hear it. I don't want to know. I don't want my girls upset....* 99

Kitty Hart-Moxon, Polish Jewish girl, adopted by relatives in the U.K.

Focus on Eva Mozes Kor

Eva Mozes and her twin sister Miriam were born in Portz, Romania in 1934. The Mozes family was transported to Simleu Silvaniei ghetto in 1944, and then to Auschwitz-Birkenau. Their experience at the hands of Dr. Mengele made the girls seriously ill, but through sheer determination they survived. Following liberation, they lived for a time in refugee camps before moving back to Romania, and in 1950, they emigrated to Israel. Here, Eva met her American husband, Michael Kor. In 1960, Eva and Michael moved to the United States.

▲ Each year, thousands of young people join with Holocaust survivors on the March of the Living. They commemorate the Holocaust by marching silently along the path from Auschwitz to Birkenau.

A NEW LIFE

Many of the surviving children of the Holocaust faced years of hardship as they struggled to adapt to living in a new country with an unfamiliar language and culture.

" *Nobody really talked about the war ... that was a taboo subject. I don't think I wanted to talk about it. I wanted very much to be accepted. Because if they knew, would they want to ... play with me? So I really didn't want them to know: I wanted to ride a bicycle and play with a doll and run. I remember one day there was a girl ... and she was climbing on a monkey-bar and her hair was blowing in the wind ... I guess I was about ten and a half then and I remember thinking: Isn't it wonderful to be climbing on a monkey-bar and to have your hair blowing in the wind, and being so free!* "

Rina Quint, Polish Jewish child survivor, New York, U.S.

THE BOYS

After the war, the British government agreed to take in 732 orphaned survivors of the Holocaust. They were known as "the Boys," though they also included girls, and they were settled in different parts of the U.K.

> 66 *Well, the group of us known as 'the Boys' came to England by plane.... I saw this very tall officer who was talking from the side of his mouth, emitting these very quick sounds and I thought: I will never learn this language.... There was a tea reception, not a single slice of black bread, all beautifully white. We hadn't seen that before. I thought: we have come to a country of milk and honey.* 99

Roman Halter, Polish Jewish teenager.

▲ Gerald and Robert Finaly, born to Jewish parents who died in the Holocaust, were then baptized as Christians. They are pictured here in 1953 after being reunited with their aunt. It had taken her eight years to win custody of the boys from the Catholic Church.

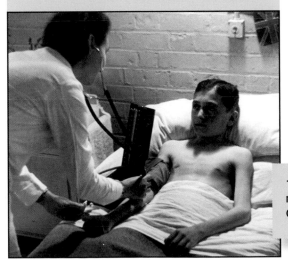

◄ A young Holocaust survivor receives medical care at a camp in England, run by the Central British Jewish Relief Fund.

CHAPTER 7

M-MURI-E A D CONSEQUENCES

ANTI-SEMITISM DID NOT END WITH THE DEFEAT OF THE NAZIS, and hundreds of Jews were murdered in eastern Europe after the war ended. Many Jewish survivors feared returning to their former homes, deciding instead to settle in western Europe, Palestine, or the U.S.

BIRTH OF ISRAEL

During the post-war years, demands grew for the establishment of a Jewish state in Palestine—a place where Jews could live without fear of persecution. Jews had been settling in Palestine since the 1890s. But their arrival was causing a serious conflict with the Palestinians already living there. By the time the British rulers of Palestine departed in 1948 and the Jews declared the founding of the state of Israel, the new country was in the midst of a full-scale war. Although Israel's establishment was controversial, it became a beacon of hope for Jews around the world following the Holocaust, and many went to live there.

SEEKING JUSTICE

The victorious powers decided that the Nazis should be punished for the crimes of the Holocaust. A series of trials were conducted in the German city of Nuremberg. Between 1945 and 1949, over 200 senior Nazis were tried, many of whom were sentenced to imprisonment or death. Hundreds of other Nazis tried to evade justice by fleeing abroad, especially to South America. A few were hunted down, notably a high-ranking Nazi named Adolf Eichmann, whose trial in Israel in 1960 caused an international sensation.

REMEMBERING THE HOLOCAUST

After the war, Jewish survivors of the Holocaust tended to remain silent about their experiences. The Eichmann trial in 1960 helped raise public awareness of the Holocaust, as did the television mini-series, *Holocaust*, in the 1970s. Today, there are memorials to the Holocaust in cities across the U.S. and Europe, and millions of people visit the major Holocaust museums each

▲ Nazi defendants pictured in the dock during the Nuremberg Trials.

year. The Holocaust is remembered in memoirs, works of art, documentaries and Hollywood films. The anniversary of the liberation of Auschwitz, January 27, has been declared Holocaust Memorial Day. In commemorating the Holocaust in these ways, we honor the memory of the millions who died, and we are reminded to remain vigilant, so that we can act to prevent genocides and mass atrocities in the future.

THE UNIVERSAL DECLARATION OF HUMAN RIGHTS

In the wake of the Holocaust, governments agreed on the need to establish and protect certain fundamental human rights, in the hope that this might help prevent future genocides. In 1948, the United Nations proclaimed the Universal Declaration of Human Rights (UDHR). It includes the right to life, liberty, and security of person.

TIMELINE

January 30, 1933 Adolf Hitler is appointed Chancellor of Germany.

April 25, 1933 Restrictions are placed on the number of Jewish children allowed to attend German schools and universities.

1933–1935 Jewish children are banned from taking part in "Aryan" sports clubs, school orchestras, and other activities. They are banned from playgrounds, swimming pools, and parks in many German towns and cities. In schools it is taught that "non-Aryans" are racially inferior.

September 1935 The Nuremberg Laws strip German Jews of their citizenship.

March 13, 1938 Germany annexes Austria.

November 9–10, 1938 *Kristallnacht*: Nazi-organized anti-Jewish riots take place throughout Germany.

November 15, 1938 Jewish children are expelled from German schools and can only attend separate Jewish schools.

December 2, 1938 The first party of *Kinderstransport* children travel to Britain.

December 8, 1938 Jews can no longer attend college.

March 15, 1939 Germany invades Czechoslovakia.

September 1, 1939 Germany invades Poland and World War II begins.

November 23, 1939 Polish Jews are ordered to wear a Star of David on their chests or as an armband.

November 28, 1939 The first Polish ghetto is established.

April 30, 1940 The Lodz ghetto is sealed off, trapping around 230,000 Jews.

November 15, 1940 The Warsaw ghetto is sealed off, trapping around 500,000 Jews.

September 1, 1941 German Jews above the age of six are forced to wear the Star of David.

January 1942 Gas chambers begin operating at Birkenau, the extermination center at Auschwitz-Birkenau.

June 1942 The German government closes all Jewish schools.

June 1, 1942 Treblinka death camp opens. Jews in France and the Netherlands are forced to wear the Star of David.

July 1942 Around 74,000 French Jews, including 11,000 children, are transported to the death camps at Auschwitz-Birkenau, Majdanek, and Sobibor.

July 19, 1942 Operation Reinhard—the mass deportation of Polish Jews to the extermination centers—begins.

September 5–12, 1942 Around 15,000 Jews in the Lodz ghetto, mostly children under ten and the elderly, are deported to the extermination center at Chelmno.

April–May 1943 The Warsaw ghetto uprising.

June 1943 The Nazis order the destruction of all the ghettos in Poland and the Soviet Union.

Late 1943 Death camps are closed.

March 1944 German forces invade Hungary.

May 15, 1944 The Nazis begin deporting Hungarian Jews. Over 430,000 are sent to Auschwitz-Birkenau, where most are gassed.

July 24, 1944 Soviet forces liberate Majdanek camp.

January 17, 1945   The Nazis evacuate Auschwitz-Birkenau and begin a "death march" back to Germany.

January 27, 1945   Soviet forces liberate Auschwitz.

April 30, 1945   Adolf Hitler commits suicide.

May 7, 1945   Germany surrenders, ending World War II in Europe.

GLOSSARY

Allied forces   The military forces of the Allies, the group of nations including Britain and the U.S. that fought against Nazi Germany and its allies during World War II.

annex   Add (territory) to one's own.

anti-Semitism   Hostility toward Jews.

Aryan   According to Nazi theory, a person of the Germanic race.

assassinate   Murder (an important person) in a surprise attack for political or religious reasons.

atrocity   An extremely wicked or cruel act.

black market   Illegal trade.

caricature   A picture that exaggerates features to make it look funny or grotesque.

circumcise   To cut off the foreskin (the roll of skin covering the end of the penis) of a young boy. Circumcision is carried out as a religious custom in Judaism.

civil rights   The rights of citizens to political and social freedom and equality under the law.

concentration camp   A place where large numbers of people are imprisoned in a relatively small area with inadequate facilities, often to provide forced labor or to await execution.

crematorium   A place where dead bodies are burned to ashes.

Czechoslovakia   A former country in eastern Europe, now divided between the Czech Republic and Slovakia.

deportation   The explusion of a foreigner from a country.

dysentery   An infection of the intestines that causes severe diarrhea.

gas chamber   An airtight room that can be filled with poisonous gas as a means of execution.

ghetto   A part of a city, especially a slum area, occupied by a minority ethnic group.

lice   Small, wingless insects that live on the skin of mammals (including humans) and birds.

malnutrition   Lack of proper nutrition, due to not eating enough of the food needed for health and growth.

Nazi Party   The National Socialist German Workers' (Nazi) Party was a German political party that existed from 1920 to 1945. It was fiercely anti-Semitic, and believed in a strong Germany and the superiority of the "Aryan" race.

partisan   A member of an armed group formed to fight secretly against an occupying force. Partisans were active in all the countries occupied by the Nazis during World War II.

persecution Hostility and ill treatment, especially toward an ethnic or religious minority.

pogrom An organized attack on an ethnic group, especially Jews in eastern Europe or Russia.

propaganda Biased information used to promote a particular political viewpoint.

Soviet Union A former country made up of Russia and a number of other countries in Central Asia. It existed from 1922 to 1991.

SS An abbreviation of Schutzstaffel (German for "defense squadron"), founded by the Nazis in 1925 to act as a personal bodyguard for Adolf Hitler. The SS later became a major security force for the Nazis and administered the concentration camps.

synagogue A building where Jews meet for worship.

typhoid fever An infectious disease that causes an outbreak of red spots on the chest and stomach, and severe irritation of the intestines.

typhus An infectious disease that causes a purple rash, headaches, and fever. It is transmitted by creatures such as lice, ticks, mites, and rat fleas.

unsanitary Lacking sewage facilities and clean drinking water.

visa Official approval, usually in the form of a stamp on a passport, allowing someone to enter, leave, or stay for a period of time in a country.

FURTHER INFORMATION

Books

Nonfiction

Auschwitz: Voices from the Death Camp (The Holocaust Through Primary Sources) by James Deem (Enslow Publishers, 2011)

The Diary of a Young Girl by Anne Frank (Puffin, 2007) [first published in the U.K. in 1952]

Erika's Story by Ruth Vander Zee (Creative Paperbacks, 2013)

Helga's Diary: A Young Girl's Account of Life in a Concentration Camp by Helga Weiss (Penguin, 2014)

Nicholas Winton and the Rescued Generation by Muriel Emanuel and Vera Gissing (Vallentine Mitchell, 2001)

Rescuing the Children: The Story of the Kindertransport by Deborah Hodge (Tundra, 2012)

Terezín: Voices from the Holocaust by Ruth Thomson (Franklin Watts, 2013)

Why Did the Holocaust Happen? (Moments in History) by Sean Sheehan (Wayland, 2013)

Fiction

The Book Thief by Markus Zusak (Picador, 2006)

The Boy in the Striped Pyjamas by John Boyne (David Fickling, 2006)

I am David by Anne Holm (Egmont, 2000) [first published 1963]

Now by Morris Gleitzman (Puffin, 2010)

Number the Stars by Lois Lowry (HarperCollins, 2011) [first published 1989]

The War Within These Walls by Aline Sax (Eerdmans, 2013)

When Hitler Stole Pink Rabbit by Judith Kerr (HarperCollins, 2008) [first published 1971]

Websites

http://archive.adl.org/children_holocaust/children_main.asp
This section of the Anti-Defamation League (ADL) website contains accounts by child survivors of the Holocaust.

www.bethshalom.com
The website of Beth Shalom, the Holocaust Memorial and Education Center.

http://holocaust.umd.umich.edu
The Voice/Vision Holocaust Survivor Oral History Archive contains a wealth of first-hand survivor accounts.

www.ushmm.org/museum/exhibit/online/phistories/
This section of the United States Holocaust Memorial Museum (USHMM) website contains eyewitness accounts of people, including children, caught up in the Holocaust.

www.yadvashem.org
The website of Yad Vashem, an international center dedicated to documenting, researching, commemorating, and educating people about the Holocaust.

Note to parents and teachers

Every effort has been made by the publishers to ensure that the websites in this book are suitable for children, that they are of the highest educational value, and that they contain no inappropriate or offensive material. However, because of the nature of the Internet, it is impossible to guarantee that the contents of these sites will not be altered. We strongly advise that Internet access is supervised by a responsible adult.

INDEX

PICTURE CREDITS